MENSA

MIGHTY MIND BENDERS

BOOST YOUR IQ

MENSA
PUBLICATIONS
MIGHTY MIND BENDERS

BOOST YOUR
IQ

HAROLD GALE & CAROLYN SKITT

CHARTWELL
BOOKS, INC.

THIS IS A CARLTON BOOK

This edition produced for Book Sales Inc.

Text and puzzles © Mensa Limited 1994
Design and artwork © Carlton Books Limited 1994

ISBN 0-7858-0130-8

Designed by FKD

Printed in Italy

CONTENTS

Introduction	**7**
Test 1	**8**
Test 2	**16**
Test 3	**24**
Test 4	**34**
Test 5	**44**
Test 6	**59**
Rainbow Test	**65**
Test 7	**90**
Test 8	**105**
Answers	**120**

INTRODUCTION

Intelligence, to a greater or lesser degree, is found in all humans. Your level of intelligence is the same throughout your life. Many people, however, fail to reach their true potential and this is the rationale behind this book.

The tests in the book are fun I.Q. tests. They begin on an easy plane but gradually rise to a more difficult one. The tests measure speed and accuracy of thought and should be regarded as a form of mental jogging. Many people take physical exercise but not so many mental exercise. Now is your chance.

Carolyn Skitt and I have put together this series of puzzles for your amusement. In each of the tests the correct answer is to be found in one of the shapes. Proceed through each test as quickly as possible and first answer those questions you find easiest. Then return to the more difficult ones. Check your answers when the time is up, total the correct answers and then find your fun I.Q. score from the table.

In the more difficult tests the fun I.Q. table indicates whether you have reached Mensa level. If you have attained the standard or risen higher, you ought to apply to join. For an accurate I.Q. rating write to Mensa, Freepost (BYI), Wolverhampton, WV2 1BR.

Mensa is the international high I.Q. society with over 110,000 members worldwide. The biggest national Mensas are to be found in the United States of America and British Isles. It is a society where people from every walk of life, every race, every creed and every political viewpoint meet and talk in friendship.

Whatever your score in these tests, it is always a good idea to find out what your real I.Q. is – after all, we measure our bodies, why not our minds?

Harold Gale
Executive Director of British Mensa

TEST 1

1 Which of the numbers should replace the question mark?

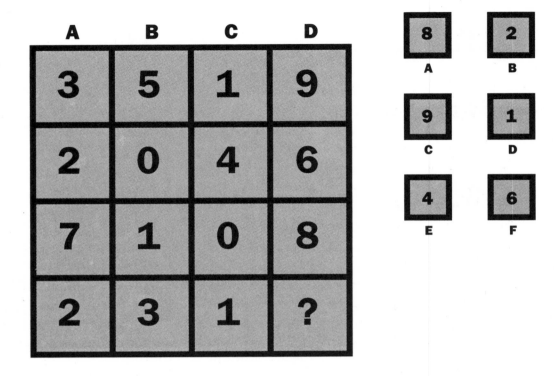

2 Each same symbol has a value. Work out the logic and discover what should replace the question mark.

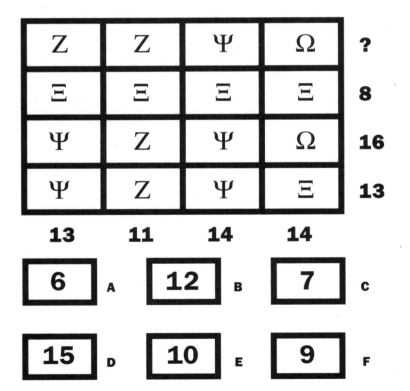

TEST 1 time limit 20 minutes

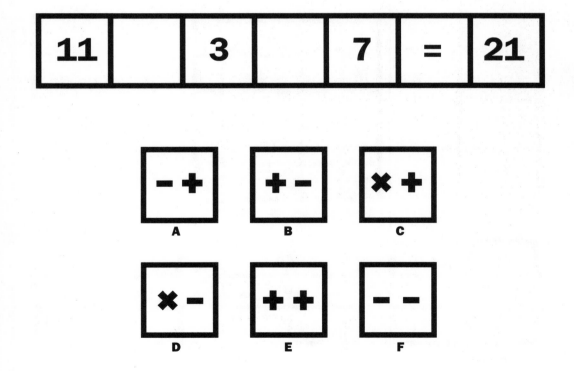

3 Here is an unusual safe. Each of the buttons must be pressed only once in the correct order to open it. The last button is marked F. The number of moves and the direction is marked on each button. Thus 1U would mean one move up, while 1L would mean one move to the left. Using the grid reference, which button is the first you must press?

4 Insert the correct mathematical signs between each number in order to resolve the equation. What are the signs?

TEST 1 time limit 20 minutes

TEST 1

5 Which triangle continues this series?

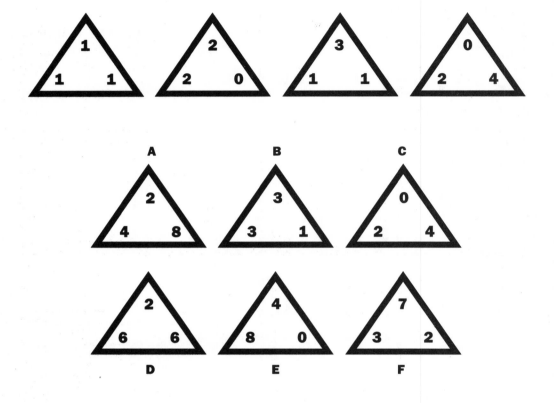

6 Discover the connection between the letters and the numbers. Which number should replace the question mark?

G	7
M	13
U	21
J	10
W	?

14	23	9
A	B	C
26	2	11
D	E	F

7 Which of the constructed boxes cannot be made from the pattern?

TEST 1

8 Which of the numbers should replace the question mark?

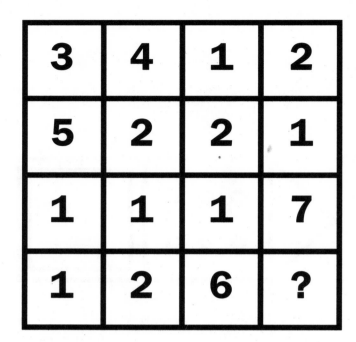

9 Which of the clocks continues this series?

(2) A (5) B
(7) C (6) D
(4) E (9) F

10 When rearranged the shapes will give a number. Which of the numbers is it?

4	2	4	2	4
2	4	4	4	2
4	4	2	2	4
2	4	2	4	2
2	4	2	2	2

11 Move from ring to touching ring, starting from the bottom left corner and finishing in the top right corner. Collect nine numbers and total them. Which is the highest possible total?

(36) A   (16) B   (18) C   (45) D   (29) E   (32) F

TEST 1 time limit 20 minutes

13

TEST 1

12 This square follows a logical pattern. Which of the tiles should be used to complete the square?

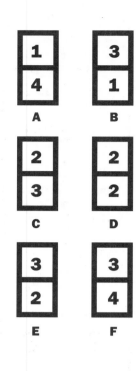

13 Which of the slices should be used to complete the cake?

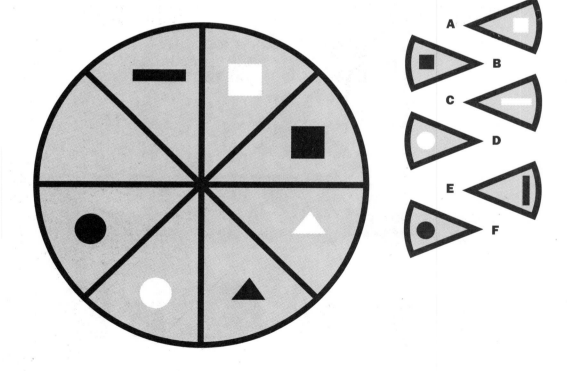

5 | 2 | | 2 | 5
1 | | ? | | 1
5 | 8 | 4 | | 3
  | 2 | 2 | 2 | 8
3 | 2 | 2 | 10 | 3

4
A

1
B

3
C

6
D

5
E

2
F

14 Each straight line of five numbers should total 20. Which of the numbers will replace the question mark?

4   3   6   1   5   8
A   B   C   D   E   F

15 Start at any corner and follow the lines. Collect another four numbers and total the five. One of the numbers in the squares below can be used to complete the diagram. If the correct one has been chosen, one of the routes involving it will give a total of 28. Which one is it?

TEST 1 time limit 20 minutes

TEST 2

1 Which of the boxes should be used to replace the question mark?

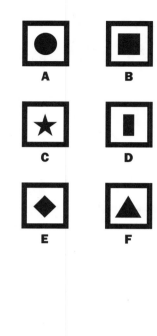

2 Scales one and two are in perfect balance. Which of these pans should replace the empty one?

TEST 2 time limit 20 minutes

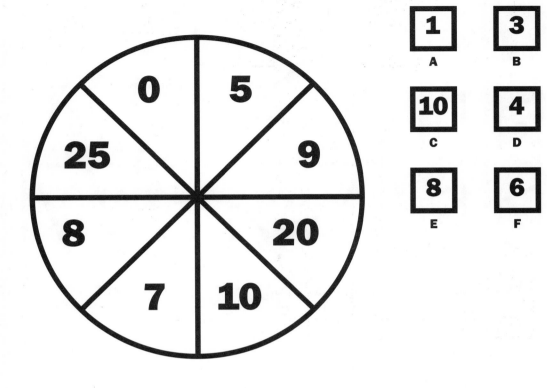

1 A

3 B

10 C

4 D

8 E

6 F

3 How many ways are there to score 25 on this dartboard using three darts only? Each dart always lands in a sector and no dart falls to the floor.

	A	B	C	D	
1	A ... A B	A B ... C	D ... D D	D ... C A	
2	B ... A D	A ... A A	C ... C D	B ... B B	
3	B C ... C	B ... B A	C C ... C	A ... B D	
4	C D ... D	A ... C D	D C ... B	B ... B C	

A3 A

B2 B

D4 C

C2 D

B4 E

A1 F

4 Which square's contents matches D1?

TEST 2 time limit 20 minutes

TEST 2

5 Which of the numbers should logically replace the question mark in the octagon?

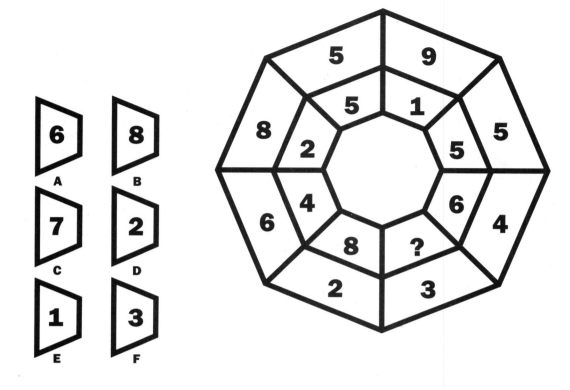

6 Which number is missing from this series?

TEST 2 time limit 20 minutes

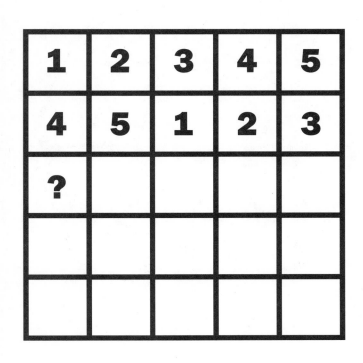

1	2	3	4	5
4	5	1	2	3
?				

1
A

5
B

2
C

3
D

4
E

7 Complete the square using the five numbers shown. When completed no row, column or diagonal line will use the same number more than once. What should replace the question mark?

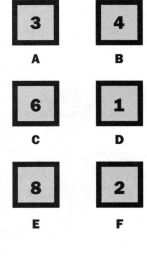

3
A

4
B

6
C

1
D

8
E

2
F

8 Which of the numbers should replace the question mark?

6	3	1	4	9
5	1	0	2	8
1	2	1	2	?

TEST 2 time limit 20 minutes

TEST 2

9 Start at 1 and move from circle to touching circle. Collect four numbers each time. How many different routes are there to collect 11? A reversed route counts twice.

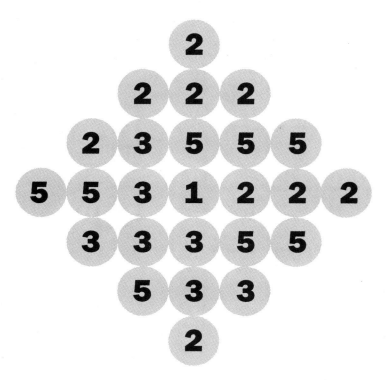

2	3
A	**B**
6	4
C	**D**
5	7
E	**F**

10 Here is an unusual safe. Each of the buttons must be pressed only once in the correct order to open it. The last button is marked F. The number of moves and the direction is marked on each button. Thus 1i would mean one move in, whilst 1o would mean one move out. 1c would mean one move clockwise and 1a would mean one move anti-clockwise. Which button is the first you must press?

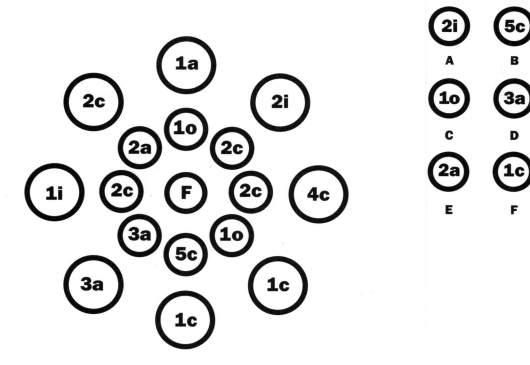

2i	5c
A	**B**
1o	3a
C	**D**
2a	1c
E	**F**

11 Which of the numbers should replace the question mark?

12 Which triangle continues this series?

TEST 2 time limit 20 minutes

TEST 2

13 Insert the correct mathematical signs between each number in order to resolve the equation. What are the signs?

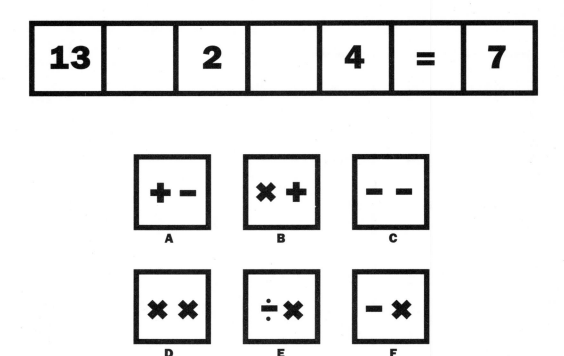

14 Discover the connection between the letters and the numbers. Which number should replace the question mark?

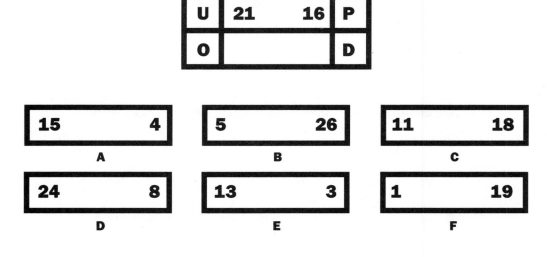

15 Which of the constructed boxes can be made from the pattern?

TEST 3

1 Each same symbol has a value. Work out the logic and discover what should replace the question mark.

α	α	α	α	**16**
β	β	δ	χ	**?**
δ	α	δ	α	
α	β	χ	χ	**21**
22	**25**			

25	A	21	B	27	C

28	D	29	E	23	F

2 Scales one and two are in perfect balance. Which of these pans should replace the empty one?

A **6**   B **7**
C **9**   D **3**
E **8**   F **4**

3 When rearranged the shapes will give a number. Which of the numbers is it?

6	1	7	3
2	5	2	8
3	5	5	1
4	4	1	?

A **6**   B **3**
C **4**   D **2**
E **5**   F **1**

4 Which of the numbers should replace the question mark?

TEST 3 time limit 25 minutes

TEST 3

5 Here is an unusual safe. Each of the buttons must be pressed only once in the correct order to open it. The last button is marked F. The number of moves and the direction is marked on each button. Thus 1i would mean one move in, whilst 1o would mean one move out. 1c would mean one move clockwise and 1a would mean one move anti-clockwise. Which button is the first you must press?

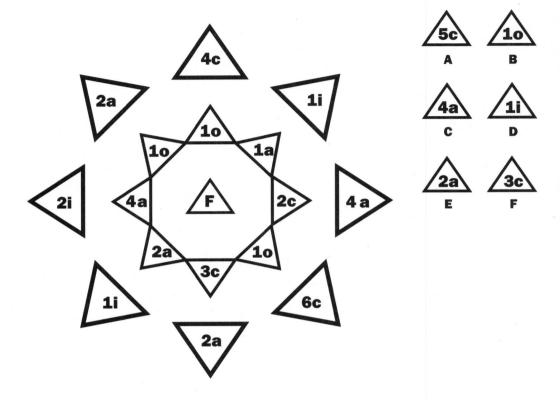

6 Which number is missing from this series?

TEST 3 time limit 25 minutes

26

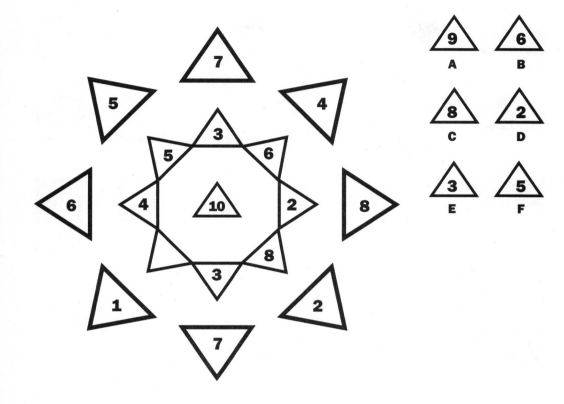

7 Which triangle should replace the empty one?

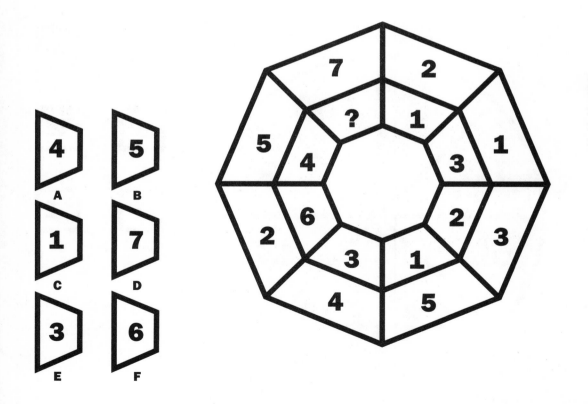

8 Which of the numbers should logically replace the question mark in the octagon?

TEST 3 time limit 25 minutes

27

TEST 3

9 Which square's contents matches C4?

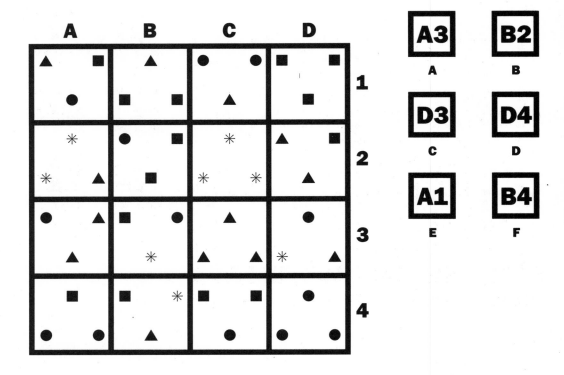

10 How many ways are there to score 123 on this dartboard using three darts only? Each dart always lands in a sector and no dart falls to the floor. Any sector can be used more than once in any set of throws, but the same set of numbers can be used in one order only.

TEST 3 time limit 25 minutes

	A	B	C	D	E	F
1	2D	4R	F	4D	3D	4D
2	3D	2D	3R	1R	3D	5L
3	5R	1U	2U	2L	1L	3L
4	3U	1R	1D	3U	1L	5L
5	1R	4U	3U	3U	2U	1U

A	B
4B	5F

C	D
2C	1E

E	F
4D	3A

11 Here is an unusual safe. Each of the buttons must be pressed only once in the correct order to open it. The last button is marked F. The number of moves and the direction is marked on each button. Thus 1U would mean one move up, while 1L would mean one move to the left. Using the grid reference, which button is the first you must press?

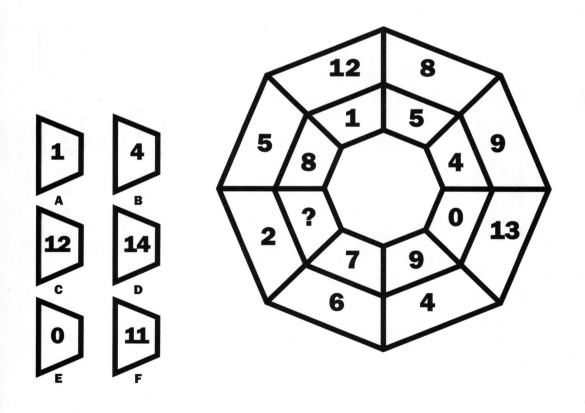

12 Which of the numbers should logically replace the question mark in the octagon?

TEST 3

13 Which of the numbers should replace the question mark?

1	0	3	4
8	4	2	6
6	2	3	7
9	5	2	?

6	9
A	**B**

5	3
C	**D**

2	7
E	**F**

14 Which of the boxes should be used to replace the question mark?

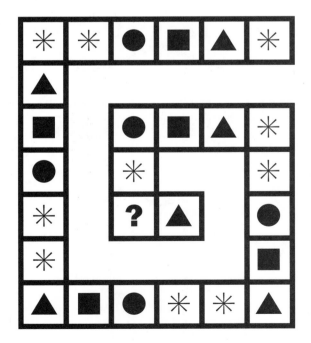

■	●
A	**B**

▲	★
C	**D**

✳	◆
E	**F**

TEST 3 time limit 25 minutes

8	1
A	**B**

7	9
C	**D**

3	4
E	**F**

15 Which of the numbers should replace the question mark?

2	1	2	1	?
5	1	2	7	3
7	2	4	8	6

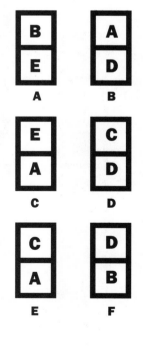

16 This square follows a logical pattern. Which of the tiles should be used to complete the square?

31

TEST 3

17 Which of the constructed boxes cannot be made from the pattern?

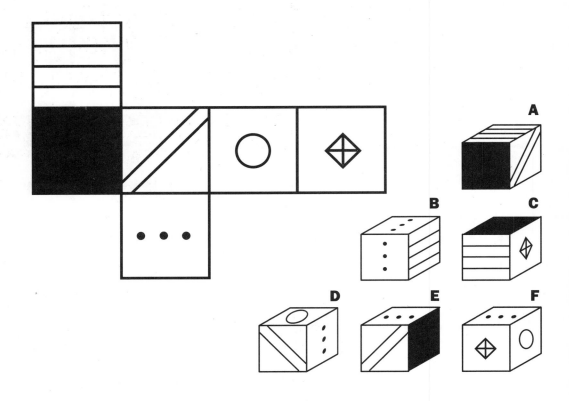

18 Move from ring to touching ring, starting from the bottom left corner and finishing in the top right corner. Collect nine numbers and total them. Which is the highest possible total?

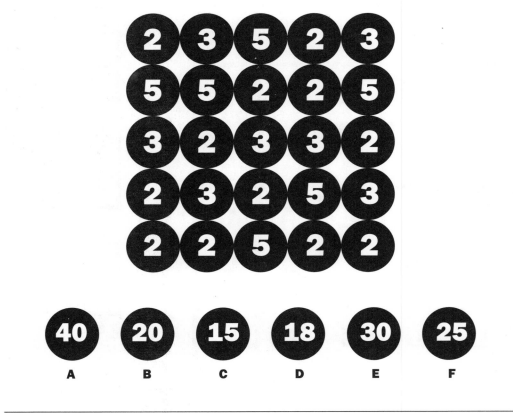

2	3	5	2	3
5	5	2	2	5
3	2	3	3	2
2	3	2	5	3
2	2	5	2	2

40	20	15	18	30	25
A	B	C	D	E	F

TEST 3 time limit 25 minutes

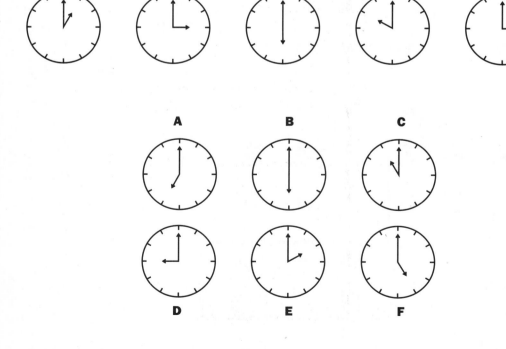

20 Which of the clocks continues this series?

TEST 3 time limit 25 minutes

TEST 4

1 Insert the correct mathematical signs between each number in order to resolve the equation. What are the signs?

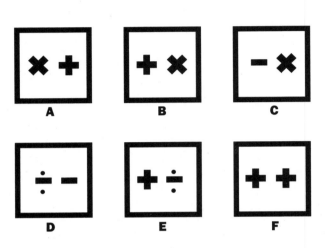

2 Start at 1 and move from circle to touching circle. Collect four numbers each time. How many different routes are there to collect 12? A reversed route counts twice.

TEST 4 time limit 25 minutes

34

3 Which triangle belongs to this series?

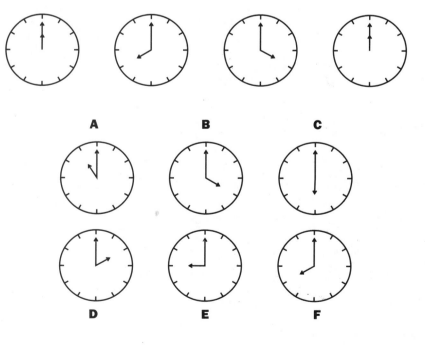

4 Which of the clocks continues this series?

TEST 4

5 Which of the numbers should replace the question mark?

6 Here is an unusual safe. Each of the buttons must be pressed only once in the correct order to open it. The last button is marked F. The number of moves and the direction is marked on each button. Thus 1U would mean one move up, while 1L would mean one move to the left. Using the grid reference, which button is the first you must press?

TEST 4 time limit 25 minutes

7 Start at any corner and follow the lines. Collect another four numbers and total the five. One of the numbers in the squares below can be used to complete the diagram. If the correct one has been chosen, one of the routes involving it will give a total of 33. Which one is it?

8 This square follows a logical pattern. Which of the tiles should be used to complete the square?

TEST 4 time limit 25 minutes

TEST 4

9 Move from ring to touching ring, starting from the bottom left corner and finishing in the top right corner. Collect nine numbers and total them. Which is the highest possible total?

A 26 B 18 C 24 D 30 E 28 F 32

10 When rearranged the shapes will give a number. Which of the numbers is it?

A 8 B 3
C 5 D 2
E 1 F 9

TEST 4 time limit 25 minutes

38

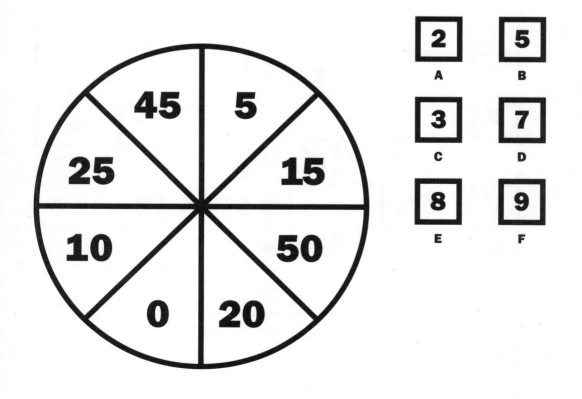

11 Which square's contents matches D1?

A. A4
B. B2
C. C1
D. C2
E. A1
F. D3

12 How many ways are there to score 60 on this dartboard using three darts only? Each dart always lands in a sector and no dart falls to the floor.

A. 2
B. 5
C. 3
D. 7
E. 8
F. 9

TEST 4 time limit 25 minutes

TEST 4

13 Each same symbol has a value. Work out the logic and discover what should replace the question mark.

α	β	α	β	18
β	χ	δ	α	
χ	χ	β	β	20
χ	δ	δ	δ	?

23   22

37 A	**30** B	**28** C
35 D	**24** E	**39** F

14 Which of the boxes should be used to replace the question mark?

TEST 4 time limit 25 minutes

40

15 Complete the square using the five numbers shown. When completed no row, column or diagonal line will use the same number more than once. What should replace the question mark?

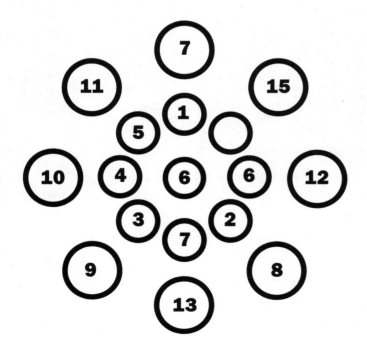

16 Which circle should replace the empty one?

TEST 4

17 Each straight line of five numbers should total 25. Which of the numbers will replace the question mark?

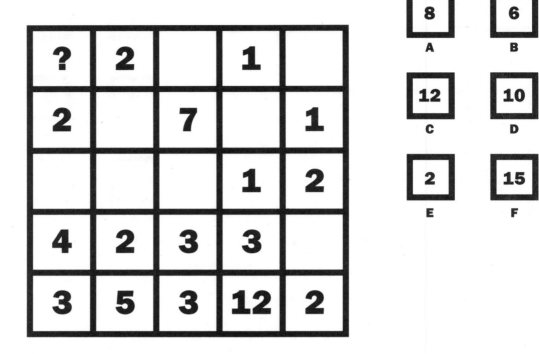

18 Which of the slices should be used to replace the question mark and complete the cake?

TEST 4 time limit 25 minutes

42

9	6
A	B

2	7
C	D

4	5
E	F

19 Which of the numbers should replace the question mark?

5	9	1	2	1
8	9	6	4	3
3	0	5	2	?

S	?	K
E	516	P
Z	262	B
I	914	N
A	120	T

20 Discover the connection between the letters and the numbers. Which number should replace the question mark?

393	671	385
A	B	C

5482	1911	2363
D	E	F

TEST 4 time limit 25 minutes

TEST 5

1 Here is an unusual safe. Each of the buttons must be pressed only once in the correct order to open it. The last button is marked F. The number of moves and the direction is marked on each button. Thus 1i would mean one move in, while 1o would mean one move out. 1c would mean one move clockwise and 1a would mean one move anti-clockwise. Which button is the first you must press?

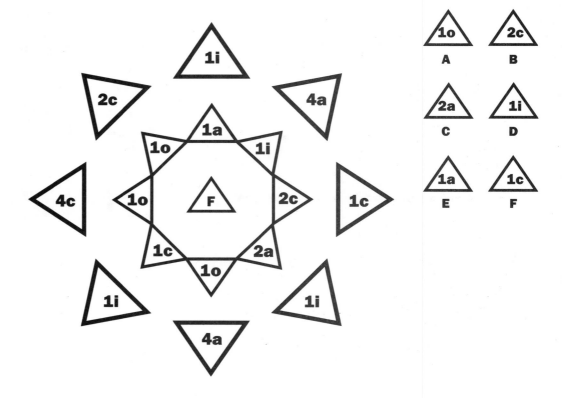

2 Complete the square using the five symbols shown. When completed no row, column or diagonal line will use the same symbol more than once. What should replace the question mark?

TEST 5 time limit 40 minutes

44

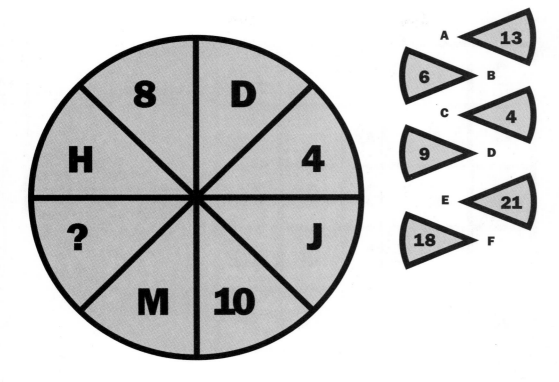

3 Which of the slices should be used to complete the cake?

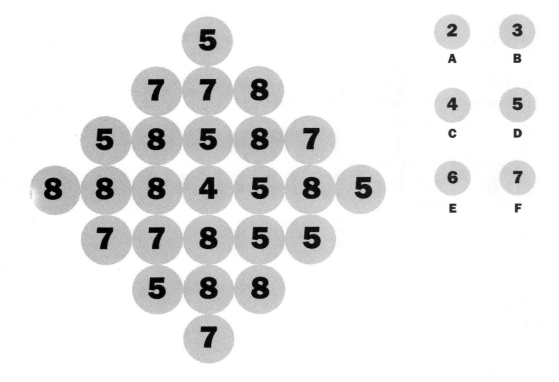

4 Start at 4 and move from circle to touching circle. Collect four numbers each time. How many different routes are there to collect 24? A reversed route counts twice.

TEST 5

5 Each straight line of five numbers should total 30. Which of the numbers will replace the question mark?

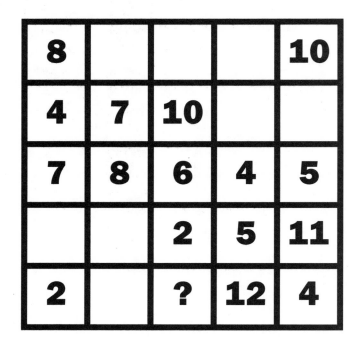

15 A	**13** B
19 C	**14** D
16 E	**3** F

6 Which number is missing from this series?

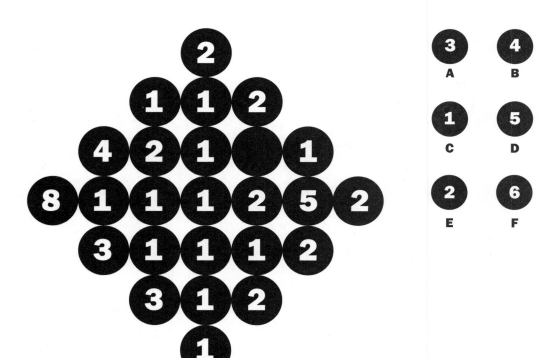

3 A	**4** B
1 C	**5** D
2 E	**6** F

TEST 5 time limit 40 minutes

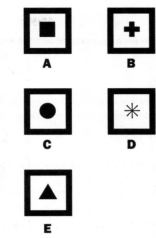

7 Complete the square using the five symbols shown. When completed no row, column or diagonal line will use the same symbol more than once. What should replace the question mark?

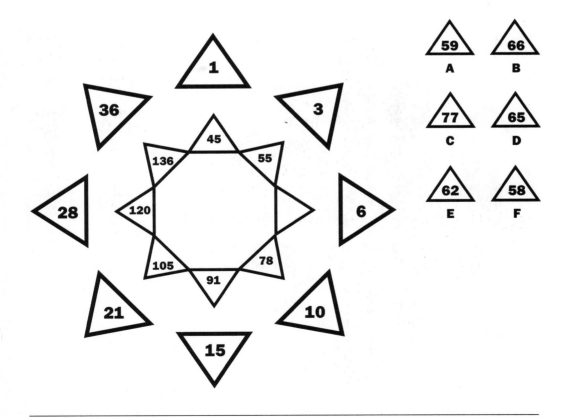

8 Which triangle should replace the empty one?

TEST 5 time limit 40 minutes

TEST 5

9 Which square's contents matches C1?

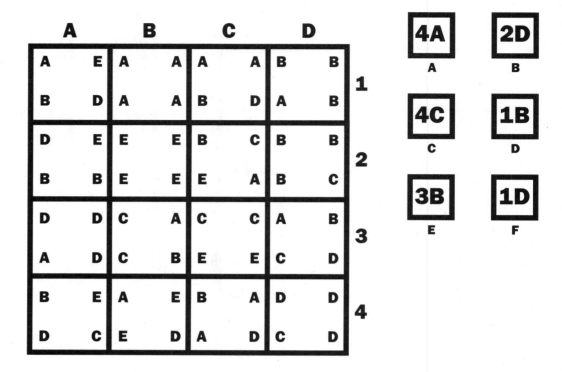

10 How many ways are there to score 62 on this dartboard using four darts only? Each dart always lands in a sector and no dart falls to the floor.

TEST 5 time limit 40 minutes

11 Which of the numbers should logically replace the question mark in the octagon?

12 This square follows a logical pattern. Which of the tiles should be used to complete the square?

TEST 5 time limit 40 minutes

TEST 5

13 Each letter has a value. Work out the logic and discover what should replace the question mark.

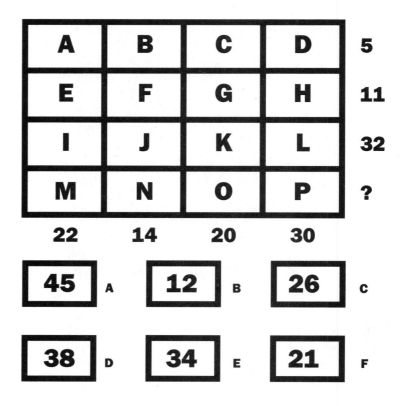

14 Here is an unusual safe. Each of the buttons must be pressed only once in the correct order to open it. The last button is marked F. The number of moves and the direction is marked on each button. Thus 1U would mean one move up, while 1L would mean one move to the left. Using the grid reference, which button is the first you must press?

TEST 5 time limit 40 minutes

50

5	5	5	6	6
6	6	6	5	4
5	6	5	5	6
4	4	4	5	5
5	4	5	6	4

49	50	55	41	47	35
A	**B**	**C**	**D**	**E**	**F**

15 Move from ring to touching ring, starting from the bottom left corner and finishing in the top right corner. Collect nine numbers and total them. Which is the highest possible total?

A	B	C	D
8	3	4	1
6	1	2	3
9	2	0	7
5	1	1	?

7	4
A	**B**
1	6
C	**D**
3	9
E	**F**

16 Which of the numbers should replace the question mark?

TEST 5 time limit 40 minutes

TEST 5

17 Start at any corner and follow the lines. Collect another four numbers and total the five. One of the numbers in the squares below can be used to complete the diagram. If the correct one has been chosen, one of the routes involving it will give a total of 20. Which one is it?

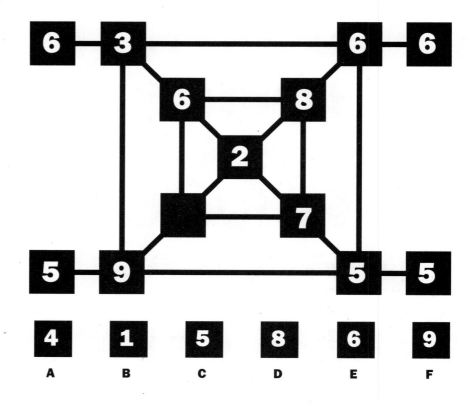

A	B	C	D	E	F
4	1	5	8	6	9

18 Scales one and two are in perfect balance. Which of these pans should replace the empty one?

19 Here is an unusual safe. Each of the buttons must be pressed only once in the correct order to open it. The last button is marked F. The number of moves and the direction is marked on each button. Thus 1i would mean one move in, while 1o would mean one move out. 1c would mean one move clock-wise and 1a would mean one move anti-clockwise. Which button is the first you must press?

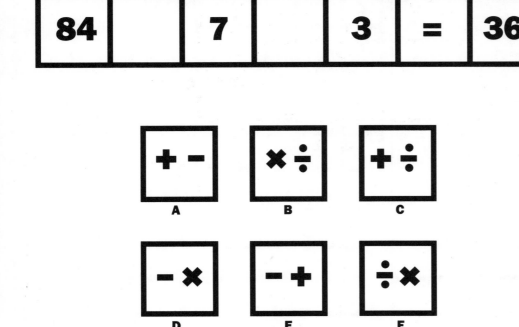

20 Insert the correct mathematical signs between each number in order to resolve the equation. What are the signs?

TEST 5 time limit 40 minutes

TEST 5

21 Which triangle belongs to this series?

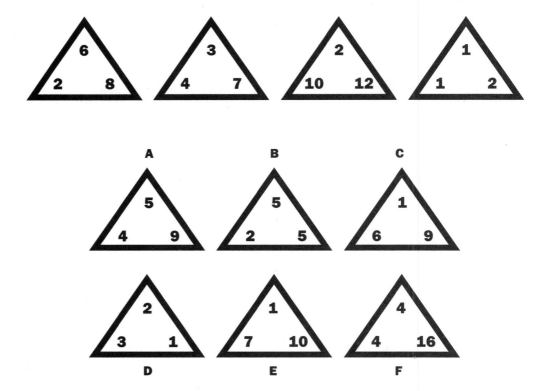

22 Discover the connection between the letters and the numbers. Which number should replace the question mark?

TEST 5 time limit 40 minutes

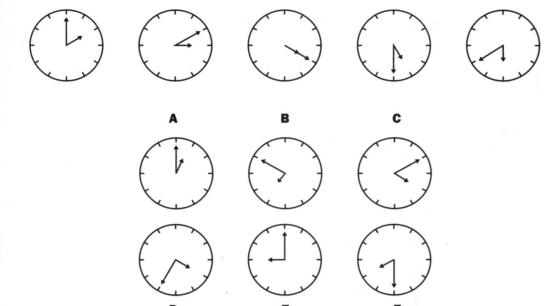

Which of the clocks continues this series?

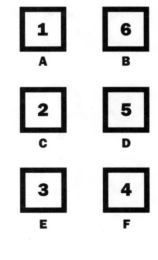

24 Which of the numbers should replace the question mark?

TEST 5

25 Which of the constructed boxes can be made from the pattern?

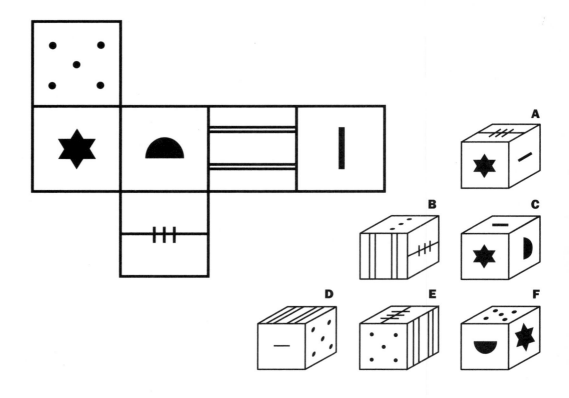

26 When rearranged the shapes will give a letter. Which of the letters is it?

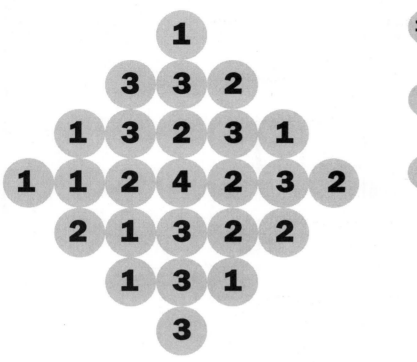

A

B 8

C 5

D 10

E 6

F 11

27 Start at 4 and move from circle to touching circle. Collect four numbers each time. How many different routes are there to collect 10? A reversed route counts twice.

12	10	14		12
7	14	14	14	1
12	18			8
11			?	21
8	2		26	8

A 6

B 4

C 12

D 10

E 8

F 2

28 Each straight line of five numbers should total 50. Which of the numbers will replace the question mark?

TEST 5 time limit 40 minutes

TEST 5

29 Which of the boxes should be used to replace the question mark?

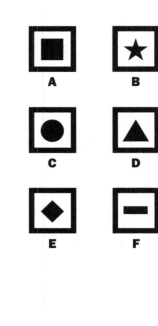

30 Each straight line of five numbers should total 35. Only two numbers must be used to complete the square. Which of the numbers will replace the question mark?

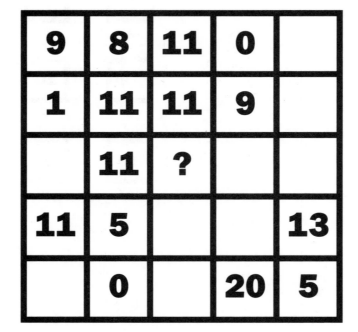

TEST 5 time limit 40 minutes

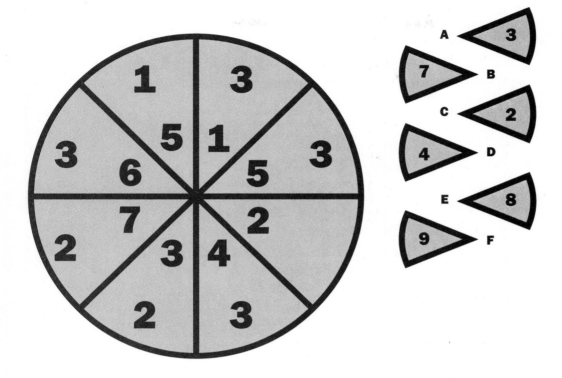

Which of the slices should be used to complete the cake?

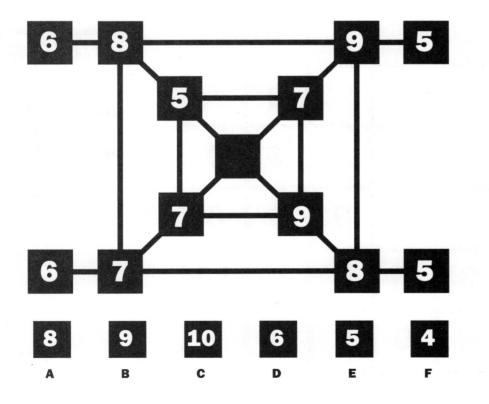

2 Start at any corner and follow the lines. Collect another four numbers and total the five. One of the numbers in the squares below can be used to complete the diagram. If the correct one has been chosen, one of the routes involving it will give a total of 41. Which one is it?

TEST 6 time limit 45 minutes

TEST 6

3 When rearranged the shapes will give a letter. Which of the letters is it?

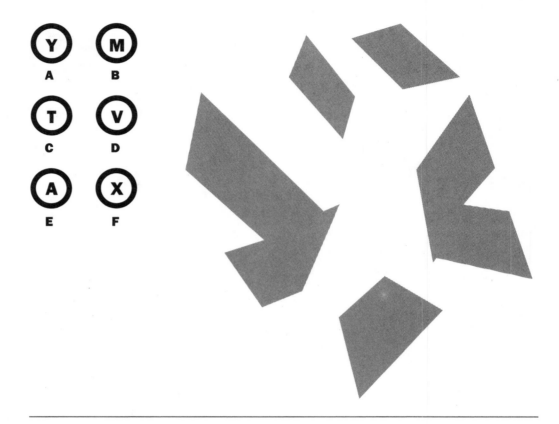

Y A	**M** B
T C	**V** D
A E	**X** F

4 Each straight line of five numbers should total 40. Only two numbers are used to complete the square. Which of the numbers will replace the question mark?

			2	
12				0
	?	8	6	6
3	7	6	7	17
6	5	6	16	7

4 A	**10** B
13 C	**21** D
18 E	**5** F

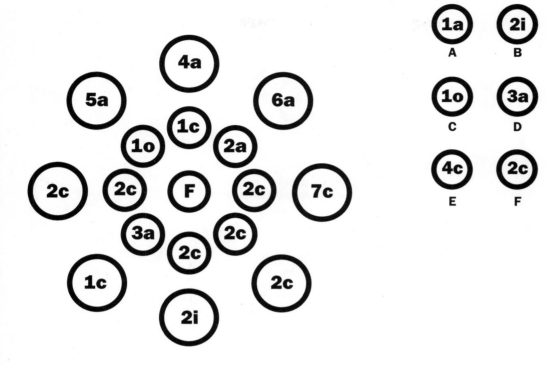

5 Here is an unusual safe. Each of the buttons must be pressed only once in the correct order to open it. The last button is marked F. The number of moves and the direction is marked on each button. Thus 1i would mean one move in, while 1o would mean one move out. 1c would mean one move clockwise and 1a would mean one move anti-clockwise. Which button is the first you must press?

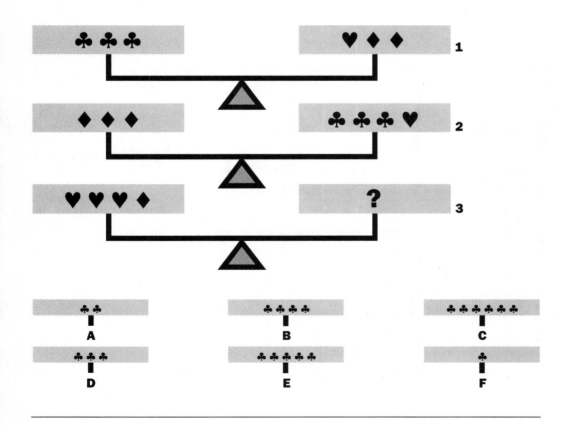

6 Scales one and two are in perfect balance. Which of these pans should replace the empty one?

TEST 6 time limit 45 minutes

TEST 6

7 Which of the slices should be used to complete the cake?

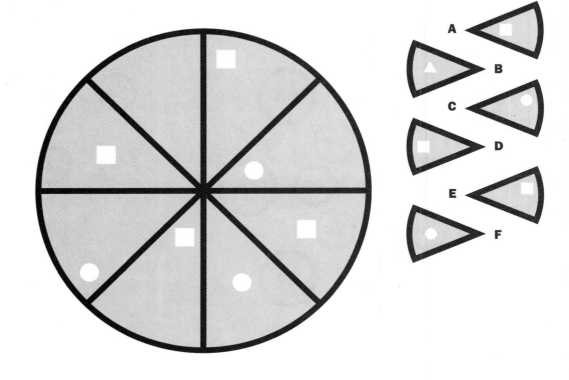

8 Which of the numbers should replace the question mark?

6	3	9	4	1
5	8	7	6	3
?	5	1	7	8

3 A	**5** B
8 C	**7** D
2 E	**0** F

TEST 6 time limit 45 minutes

9 Which arrow is missing from this series?

10 Move from ring to touching ring, starting from the bottom left corner and finishing in the top right corner. Collect nine numbers and total them. Which is the highest possible total?

TEST 6 time limit 45 minutes

TEST 6

11 This square follows a logical pattern. Which of the tiles should be used to complete the square?

TEST 6 time limit 45 minutes

12 Which square's contents matches D4?

	A		B		C		D		
1	1	5	1	3	1	1	3	**1**
5	5	2	3	2	3	5	4	
2	3	4	4	4	2	3	3	**2**
4	3	1	4	2	5	4	5	
3	3	1	4	4	4	2	5	**3**
4	3	2	5	1	1	4	3	
3	4	5	3	4	2	3	5	**4**
2	2	4	4	3	1	1	2	

- **A2** — A
- **C1** — B
- **D3** — C
- **C3** — D
- **B4** — E
- **B1** — F

RAINBOW TEST

A	B	C	D	E	F
4	7	2	3	5	4

- Pale Blue
- Dark Blue
- Pink
- Orange
- Green
- Red
- Yellow

1 Move from circle to touching circle, starting from the bottom left corner and finishing in the top right corner. Collect nine circles each time. How many different routes are there to collect four orange, three blue, one pink and one green?

2 Here is an unusual safe. Each of the buttons must be pressed only once in the correct order to open it. The last button is marked F. The number of moves is marked on each button. A black number means move down. A red number means move up. A pink number means move left and a green number means move right. Thus a red 1 would mean one move up, whilst a green 1 would mean one move to the right. Which button is the first you must press?

TEST time limit 1 hour

RAINBOW TEST

3 Which circle is missing from this series?

A

B

C

D

E

F

4 Which of the constructed boxes cannot be made from the pattern?

A

B

C

D

E

F

TEST time limit 1 hour

RAINBOW TEST

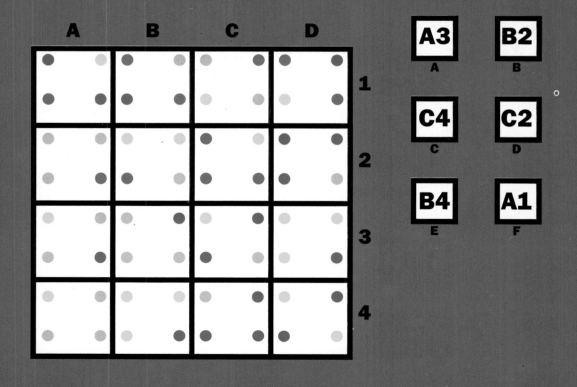

5 Start at any corner and follow the lines. Collect another four boxes. Green boxes are worth 2 each, red boxes are worth 4 and blue boxes are worth 3. Total the five boxes. What is the highest possible total?

19	16	18	15	20	17
A	B	C	D	E	F

A3 — A
B2 — B

6 Which square's contents matches B1?

C4 — C
C2 — D

B4 — E
A1 — F

TEST time limit 1 hour

RAINBOW TEST

7 A dark blue circle is worth 3, a yellow circle 4, a pink one 6, a light blue one 5 and a red one 8. Black circles are worth minus 3 each. Follow the arrows from the bottom left circle to the top right circle. Total the circles as you go. What is the lowest you can total?

6	**8**
A	B
11	**10**
C	D
12	**16**
E	F

8 Each same box has a value. Work out the logic and discover what should replace the question mark.

20 A	**26** B	**34** C
32 D	**35** E	**22** F

TEST time limit 1 hour

9 Move from circle to touching circle, starting from the bottom left corner and finishing in the top right corner. A red circle is worth minus 3, a blue one minus 1 and a green one minus 2. Collect nine circles each time and total them. How many different routes are there to total 0?

10 When the square is completed no two identical squares will appear in any row, column or diagonal line. What should replace the question mark?

TEST time limit 1 hour

RAINBOW TEST

11 Which square's contents matches C1?

12 Move from oval to touching circle, starting from the bottom left-hand corner finishing in the top right corner. A red circle is worth minus 6, a blue one minus 3, a pink one minus 4, a black one is worth minus 2 and a green one minus 7. Collect nine circles each time and total them. What is the highest number you can possibly total?

13 Here is an unusual safe. Each of the buttons must be pressed only once in the correct order to open it. The last button is marked F. The number of moves is marked on each button. A pink number means move down. A blue number means move up. A green number means move left and a red number means move right. Thus a blue 1 would mean one move up, while a green 1 would mean one move to the left. Which button is the first you must press?

14 A yellow circle is worth 3, a red circle 4, a green one 5 and an orange one 2. Black circles are worth minus 2 each. Follow the arrows from the bottom left-hand circle to the top right-handcircle. Total the circles as you go. What is the highest you can total?

8 A	**6** B
20 C	**12** D
16 E	**10** F

TEST time limit 1 hour

RAINBOW TEST

15 When the square is completed no two identical squares will appear in any row, column or diagonal line. What should replace the question mark?

16 Move from circle to touching circle, starting from the bottom left corner and finishing in the top right corner. Collect nine circles each time. How many different routes are there to collect two orange, two pink, two green, two yellow and one black?

TEST time limit 1 hour

72

17 Which of the constructed boxes can be made from the pattern?

A

B   C

D   E   F

18 Which circle is missing from this series?

A   B

C   D

E   F

TEST time limit 1 hour

RAINBOW TEST

19 Each same box has a value. Work out the logic and discover what should replace the question mark?

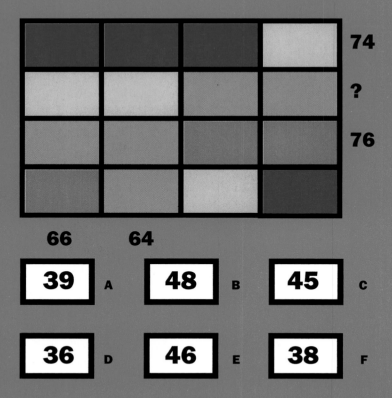

74

?

76

66   64

39 A	**48** B	**45** C
36 D	**46** E	**38** F

20 Start at any corner and follow the lines. Collect another four boxes. Green boxes are worth 4 each, pink boxes are worth 2, yellow boxes are worth 3 and dark blue boxes are worth 5. Total the five boxes. What is the highest possible total?

20	**15**	**17**	**23**	**19**	**22**
A	B	C	D	E	F

TEST time limit 1 hour

21	19	16	23	24	28
A	B	C	D	E	F

21 Move from circle to touching circle, starting from the bottom left corner and finishing in the top right corner. Collect nine circles each time. How many different routes are there to collect one orange, one red, one blue, three green and three pink?

3	1	1	2	1	5
1	5	2	2	4	4
1	1	3	1	1	4
3	4	1	3	2	1
4	1	1	2	F	2
3	2	1	2	4	4
2	4	1	5	6	1

2	3
A	B

4	6
C	D

3	3
E	F

22 Here is an unusual safe. Each of the buttons must be pressed only once in the correct order to open it. The last button is marked F. The number of moves is marked on each button. A red number means move down. A blue number means move up. A green number means move left and a pink number means move right. Thus a blue 1 would mean one move up, whilst a pink 1 would mean one move to the right. Which button is the first you must press?

TEST time limit 1 hour

RAINBOW TEST

23 Which circle is missing from this series?

24 Move from circle to touching circle, starting from the bottom left corner and finishing in the top right corner. A yellow circle is worth minus 4, a blue one minus 2, a pink one is worth minus 1 and a green one minus 3. Collect nine circles each time and total them. What is the highest number you can possibly total?

TEST time limit 1 hour

25 Which square's contents matches A2?

C1 (A)	A3 (B)
B4 (C)	D2 (D)
D1 (E)	C4 (F)

26 Start at any corner and follow the lines. Collect another four boxes. Green boxes are worth 3 each, yellow boxes are worth 4, black boxes are worth 2, a blue box is worth 6 and orange boxes are worth 5. Total the five boxes. What is the lowest possible total?

21	22	23	18	19	17
A	B	C	D	E	F

TEST time limit 1 hour

RAINBOW TEST

27 Which of the constructed boxes can be made from the pattern?

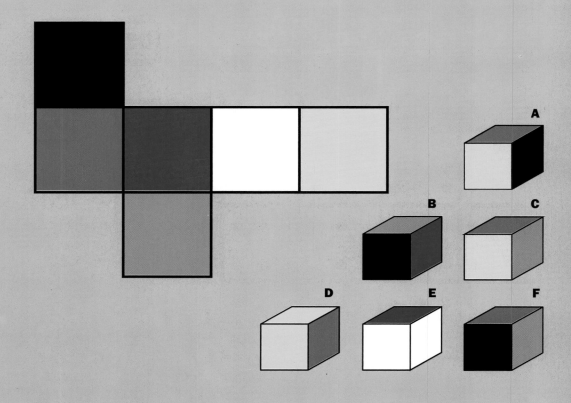

28 Each same box has a value. Work out the logic and discover what should replace the question mark.

A 30 B 31 C 28

D 29 E 26 F 25

TEST time limit 1 hour

41 A

49 B

45 C

50 D

42 E

53 F

29 A orange circle is worth 7, a red circle 8, a green one 5, a blue circle is worth 6 and a yellow one 4. Black circles are worth 5 each. Follow the arrows from the bottom left circle to the top right circle. Total the circles as you go. What is the lowest you can total?

A

B

C

D

E

30 When the square is completed no two identical squares will appear in any row, column or diagonal line. What should replace the question mark?

TEST time limit 1 hour

RAINBOW TEST ANSWERS

1 B.
2 F. Pink 2 in the third row, third column
3 D. Start at the top, the series reads red, blue, green, black and repeats from left to right.
4 E
5 C.
6 C.
7 D.
8 B. Pink =4, blue =8, green =7.
9 B.
10 A.
11 E.
12 C.
13 F. Pink 1 in the third row, second column.
14 F.
15 D.
16 D.
17 B.
18 A. Start in the extreme left circle. The series, orange, green, pink, red, blue, black, zigzags up and down.
19 E. Blue =23, orange =5, green =18, pink =20.
20 F.
21 A.
22 A. Blue 2 in the fifth row, fourth column.
23 F. Start in the top circle. The series moves across from left to right as follows: Black/white, white/black, blue/red, red/blue, green/orange, orange/green etc.
24 E.
25 F.
26 E.
27 C.
28 D. Green =6, red =4, pink =7, yellow =8.
29 C.
30 B.

SCORE	I.Q.	PERCENTILE
30	161	99
29	160	99
28	157	99
27	155	99
26	154	98
25	152	98
24	150	98
23	148	98*
20	138	95
19	136	94
18	134	93
17	132	92
16	131	91
15	130	90
14	125	85
13	122	80
12	117	75
11	115	70
10	112	65
9	108	60
8	105	55
7	100	50
6	95	45
5	90	40

* MENSA LEVEL
You should attempt to join
– see front page for details.

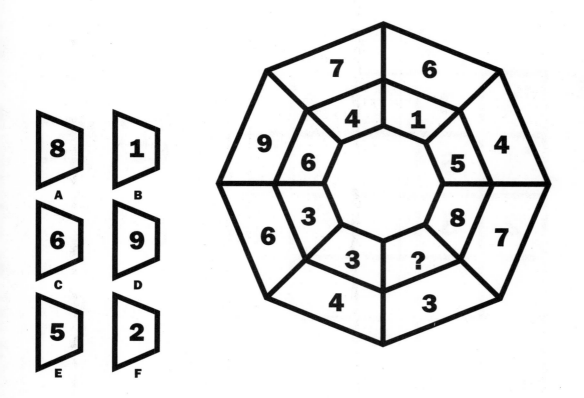

13 How many ways are there to score 85 on this dartboard using four darts only? Each dart always lands in a sector and no dart falls to the floor.

14 Which of the numbers should logically replace the question mark in the octagon?

TEST 6 time limit 45 minutes

TEST 6

15 Which circle should replace the empty one?

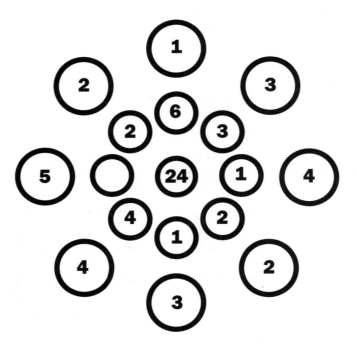

16 Complete the square using the five numbers shown. When completed no row, column or diagonal line will use the same number more than once. What should replace the question mark?

A	1	B
D	7	K
Q	2	O
R	2	T
Z	?	C

17 Discover the connection between the letters and the numbers. Which number should replace the question mark?

A	B	C
12	5	20

D	E	F
28	23	9

18 Which triangle belongs to this series?

TEST 6

19 Each same symbol has a value. Work out the logic and discover what should replace the question mark.

Κ	Κ	Λ	Λ	**46**
Λ	Κ	Κ	Ο	
Ο	Ο	Π	Π	**62**
Λ	Λ	Κ	Ο	
50	**49**		**?**	

48 A	**58** B	**50** C	
42 D	**49** E	**47** F	

20 Which of the numbers should replace the question mark?

2	3	2	8
1	8	1	9
3	0	3	3
1	1	4	?

2 A	**1** B
4 C	**5** D
8 E	**7** F

TEST 6 time limit 45 minutes

84

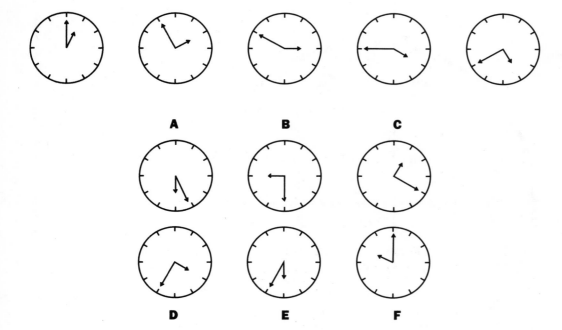

Which of the clocks continues this series?

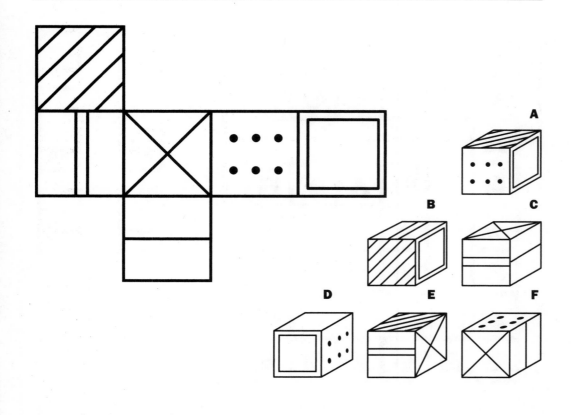

22 Which of the constructed boxes cannot be made from the pattern?

TEST 6 time limit 45 minutes

TEST 6

23 Which of the slices should be used to complete the cake?

24 Which of the boxes should be used to replace the question mark?

TEST 6 time limit 45 minutes

| 8 | | 7 | | 3 | | 1 | | 19 | = | 76 |

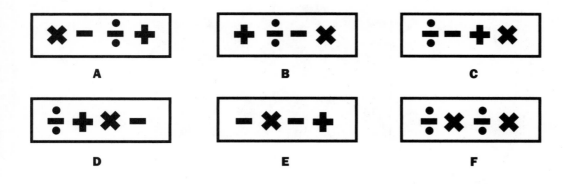

A   B   C

D   E   F

25 Insert the correct mathematical signs between each number in order to resolve the equation. What are the signs?

	A	B	C	D	E	F
1	1R	3D	1R	4D	5D	1L
2	2D	3R	1R	2D	4L	4L
3	F	1R	2U	2L	4L	2U
4	1D	4R	2D	1U	2L	2D
5	5R	1D	1L	1R	1U	2U
6	5U	2R	1U	3L	3U	4U

6B	2C
A	B

6D	3E
C	D

2F	4A
E	F

26 Here is an unusual safe. Each of the buttons must be pressed only once in the correct order to open it. The last button is marked F. The number of moves and the direction is marked on each button. Thus 1U would mean one move up, while 1L would mean one move to the left. Using the grid reference, which button is the first you must press?

TEST 6 time limit 45 minutes

TEST 6

27 Move from ring to touching ring, starting from the bottom left corner and finishing in the top right corner. Collect nine numbers and total them. Which is the highest possible total?

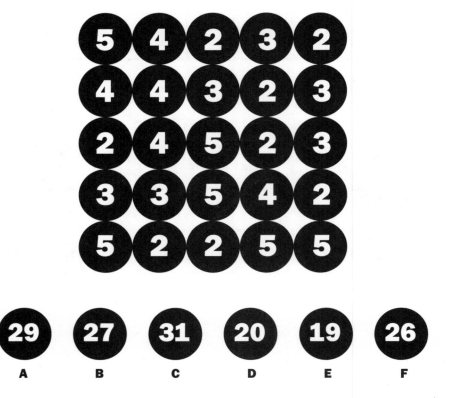

28 Which square's contents matches B1?

TEST 6 time limit 45 minutes

29 Which arrow is missing from this series?

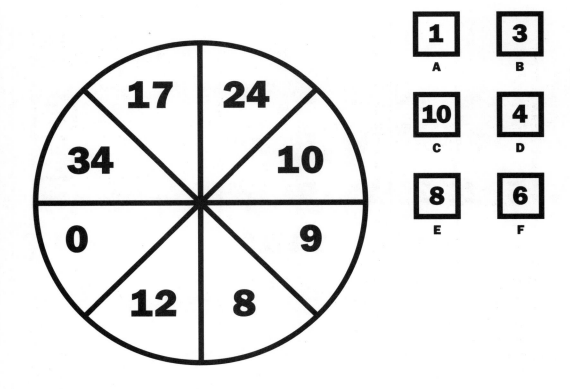

30 How many ways are there to score 58 on this dartboard using four darts only? Each dart always lands in a sector and no dart falls to the floor.

TEST 6 time limit 45 minutes

TEST 7

1 Which triangle belongs to this series?

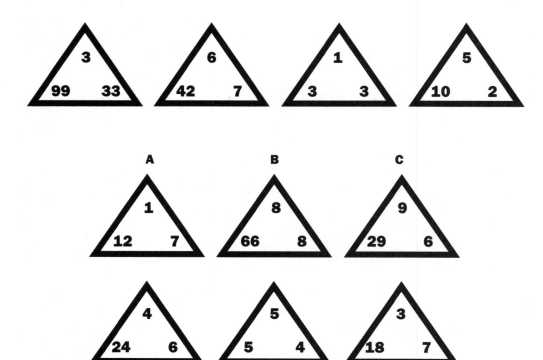

2 Start at 15 and move from circle to touching circle. Collect four numbers each time. How many different routes are there to collect 50? A reversed route counts twice.

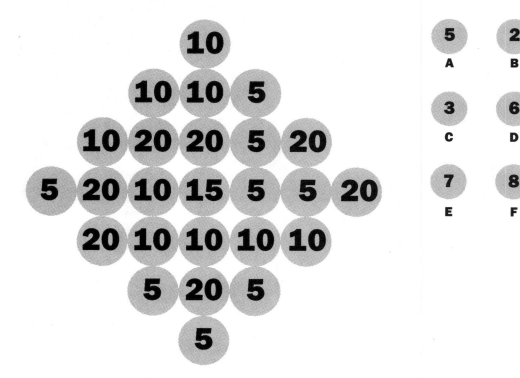

2	2	5	7	0
4	9	5	7	?
7	2	1	4	6

1 A	**3** B
8 C	**9** D
6 E	**4** F

3 Which of the numbers should replace the question mark?

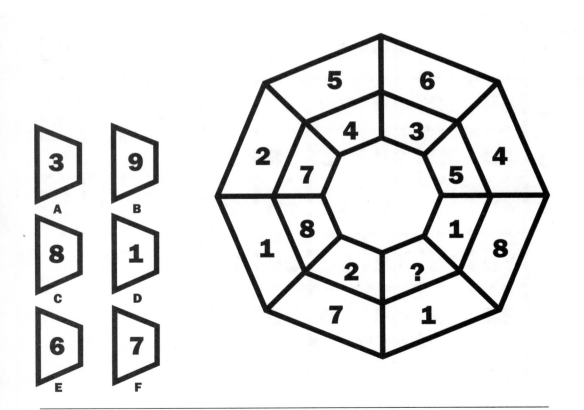

3 A	**9** B
8 C	**1** D
6 E	**7** F

4 Which of the numbers should logically replace the question mark in the octagon?

TEST 7 time limit 1 hour

91

TEST 7

5 Complete the square using the five symbols shown. When completed no row, column or diagonal line will use the same symbol more than once. What should replace the question mark?

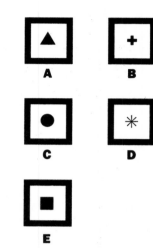

6 Here is an unusual safe. Each of the buttons must be pressed only once in the correct order to open it. The last button is marked F. The number of moves and the direction is marked on each button. Thus 1U would mean one move up, whilst 1L would mean one move to the left. Using the grid reference, which button is the first you must press?

TEST 7 time limit 1 hour

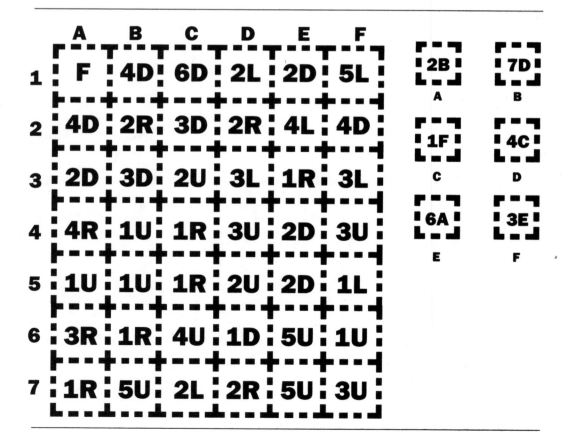

	A	B	C	D	E	F
1	F	4D	6D	2L	2D	5L
2	4D	2R	3D	2R	4L	4D
3	2D	3D	2U	3L	1R	3L
4	4R	1U	1R	3U	2D	3U
5	1U	1U	1R	2U	2D	1L
6	3R	1R	4U	1D	5U	1U
7	1R	5U	2L	2R	5U	3U

2B A	**7D** B
1F C	**4C** D
6A E	**3E** F

7 Which of the boxes should be used to replace the question mark?

8 Which of the numbers should replace the question mark?

8	4	2	2	4
9	1	1	2	2
?	2	1	0	2

TEST 7 time limit 1 hour

TEST 7

9 When rearranged the shapes will give a letter. Which of the letters is it?

A U
B W
C V
D N
E B
F C

10 When the tiles in this square are rearranged a logical pattern will emerge. Which of the tiles should be used to complete the square?

3 A	**9** B
7 C	**6** D
12 E	**11** F

11 How many ways are there to score 99 on this dartboard using five darts only? Each dart always lands in a sector and no dart falls to the floor.

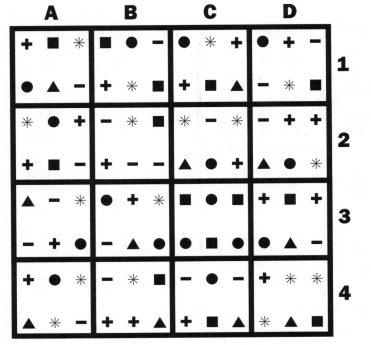

D3 A	**B4** B
C2 C	**A1** D
B1 E	**A3** F

12 Which square's contents matches A4?

TEST 7 time limit 1 hour

95

TEST 7

13 Which shape is missing from this series?

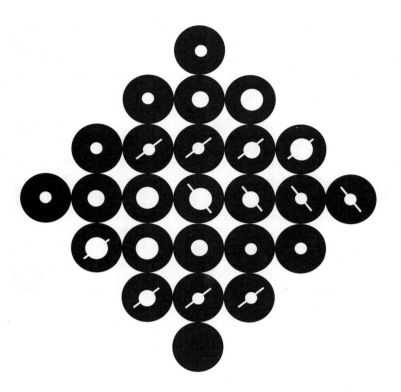

14 Which triangle should replace the empty one?

TEST 7 time limit 1 hour

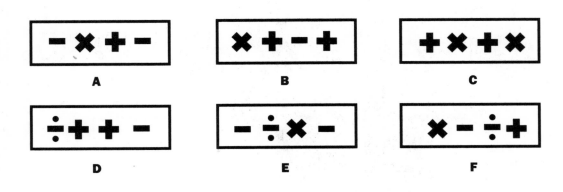

| 28 | | 4 | | 8 | | 21 | | 5 | = | 58 |

15 Insert the correct mathematical signs between each number in order to resolve the equation. What are the signs?

A   **- × + -**

B   **× + - +**

C   **+ × + ×**

D   **÷ + + -**

E   **- ÷ × -**

F   **× - ÷ +**

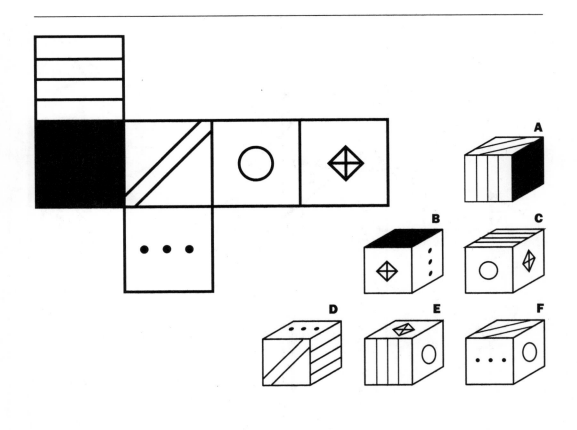

16 Which of the constructed boxes cannot be made from the pattern?

A

B   C

D   E   F

TEST 7 time limit 1 hour

TEST 7

17 Which triangle continues this series?

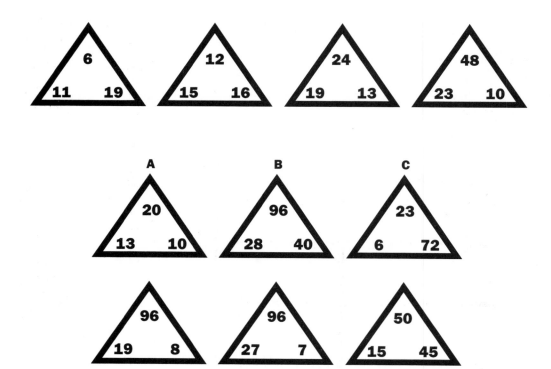

18 Which of the slices should be used to complete the cake?

TEST 7 time limit 1 hour

11	12	13	0	
8	13	13	11	0
11	13			3
6				
	0	?	24	

5 A	**2** B
3 C	**4** D
1 E	**6** F

19 Each straight line of five numbers should total 45. Which of the numbers will replace the question mark?

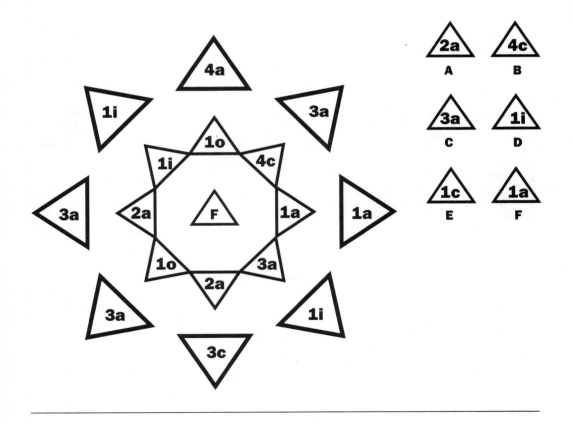

2a A	**4c** B
3a C	**1i** D
1c E	**1a** F

20 Here is an unusual safe. Each of the buttons must be pressed only once in the correct order to open it. The last button is marked F. The number of moves and the direction is marked on each button. Thus 1i would mean one move in, whilst 1o would mean one move out. 1c would mean one move clockwise and 1a would mean one move anti-clockwise. Which button is the first you must press?

TEST 7 time limit 1 hour

TEST 7

21 Each same symbol has a value. Work out the logic and discover what should replace the question mark.

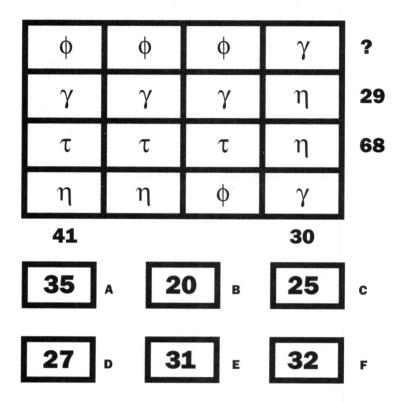

φ	φ	φ	γ	**?**
γ	γ	γ	η	**29**
τ	τ	τ	η	**68**
η	η	φ	γ	

41   **30**

35 A	**20** B	**25** C
27 D	**31** E	**32** F

22 This square follows a logical pattern. Which of the tiles should be used to complete the square?

TEST 7 time limit 1 hour

A ⑧   B ①
C ②   D ③
E ④   F ⑥

23 When rearranged the shapes will give a number. Which of the numbers is it?

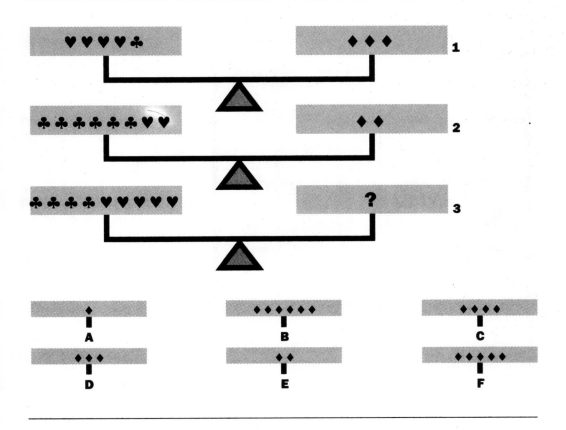

24 Scales one and two are in perfect balance. Which of these pans should replace the empty one?

TEST 7 time limit 1 hour

TEST 7

25 Start at any corner and follow the lines. Collect another four numbers and total the five. One of the numbers in the squares below can be used to complete the diagram. If the correct one has been chosen, one of the routes involving it will give a total of 45. Which one is it?

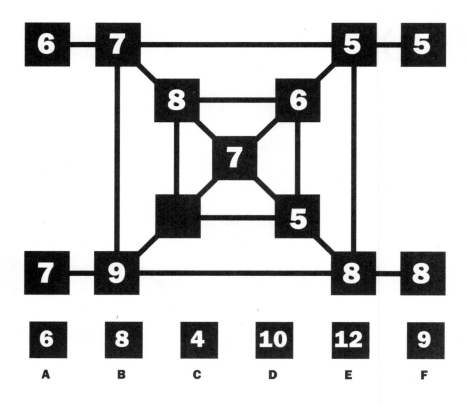

26 Which of the numbers should replace the question mark?

TEST 7 time limit 1 hour

A	B	C
+ ÷ − ×	× × ÷ ÷	÷ × − +

D	E	F
× − ÷ +	+ + − ×	− − × +

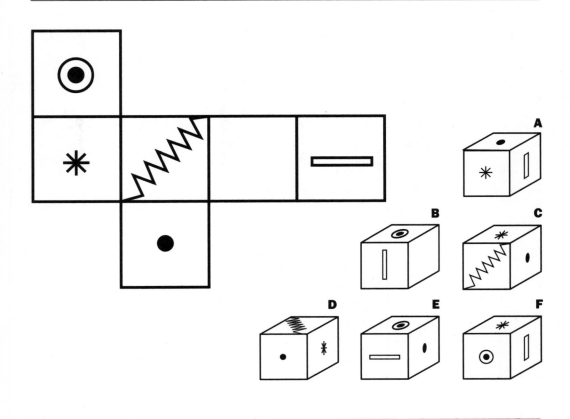

28 Which of the constructed boxes can be made from the pattern?

TEST 7 time limit 1 hour

103

TEST 7

29 Discover the connection between the letters and the numbers. Which number should replace the question mark?

F	136	M
U	421	D
H	178	Q
O	115	A
X	?	I

672	834	411
A	B	C
295	118	924
D	E	F

30 Which of the clocks continues this series?

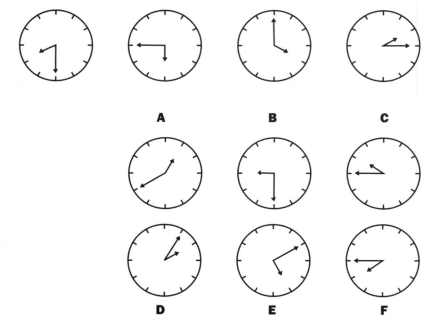

A   B   C

D   E   F

TEST 7 time limit 1 hour

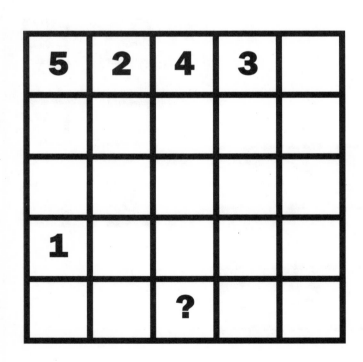

1 Which of the numbers should logically replace the question mark in the octagon?

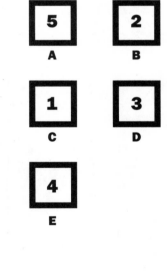

2 Complete the square using the five numbers shown. When completed no row, column or diagonal line will use the same number more than once. Which can logically replace the question mark?

TEST 8 time limit 1 hour

TEST 8

3 Start at 3 and move from circle to touching circle. Collect four numbers each time. How many different routes are there to collect 13? A reversed route counts twice.

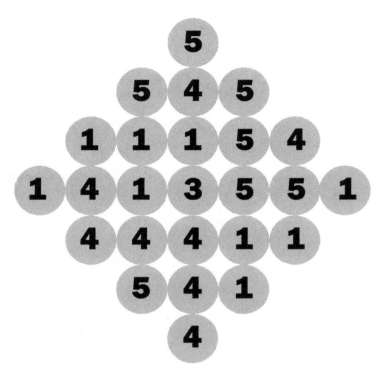

1	5
A	B
3	6
C	D
7	4
E	F

4 Which of the numbers should replace the question mark?

9	5	4	8	1
8	9	6	3	1
7	5	?	2	3

3	2
A	B
6	9
C	D
5	1
E	F

TEST 8 time limit 1 hour

5 Here is an unusual safe. Each of the buttons must be pressed only once in the correct order to open it. The last button is marked F. The number of moves and the direction is marked on each button. Thus 1i would mean one move in, while 1o would mean one move out. 1c would mean one move clockwise and 1a would mean one move anti-clockwise. Which button is the first you must press?

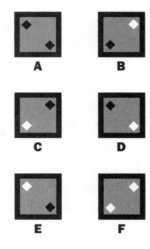

6 Which of the boxes should be used to replace the question mark?

TEST 8 time limit 1 hour

TEST 8

7 Discover the connection between the letters and the numbers. Which number should replace the question mark?

K	16
Y	2
P	11
E	22
L	?

15	13	11
A	B	C

18	8	6
D	E	F

8 Which of the clocks continues this series?

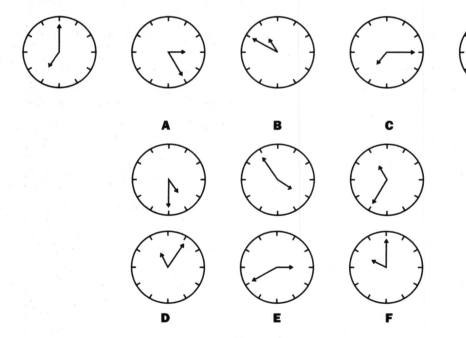

A   B   C

D   E   F

TEST 8 time limit 1 hour

TEST 8

	A	B	C	D
	7	5	3	4
	9	7	2	8
	6	8	7	2
	4	5	3	?

4	7
A	B

3	9
C	D

6	8
E	F

9 Which of the numbers should replace the question mark?

τ	ψ	η	φ	63
φ	η	ψ	ψ	
τ	τ	τ	ψ	85
η	φ	η	η	?

| 58 | 63 | 61 |

33	A	30	B	38	C

31	D	36	E	34	F

10 Each same symbol has a value. Work out the logic and discover what should replace the question mark.

TEST 8 time limit 1 hour

109

TEST 8

11 Move from ring to touching ring, starting from the bottom left corner and finishing in the top right corner. Collect nine numbers and total them. Which is the highest possible total?

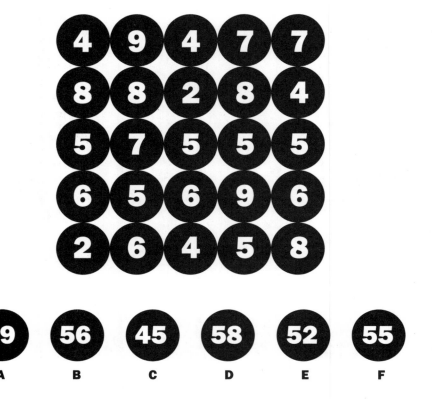

12 Scales one and two are in perfect balance. Which of these pans should replace the empty one?

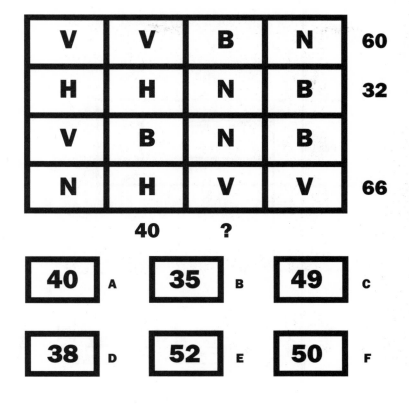

V	V	B	N	60
H	H	N	B	32
V	B	N	B	66
N	H	V	V	66

40   ?

40	A	35	B	49	C
38	D	52	E	50	F

13 Each same letter has a value. Work out the logic and discover what should replace the question mark.

	A	B	C	D	E	F
1	3R	4R	2L	2D	6D	1L
2	1R	1U	4D	2R	F	3L
3	3D	3D	1L	4D	4L	1L
4	3R	1L	1U	2R	2L	1U
5	3U	3R	1R	2L	1D	5L
6	5R	2U	5U	4U	2U	2L
7	5R	1R	2L	2L	5U	2U

2B	4E
A	B

1B	5C
C	D

6F	7D
E	F

14 Here is an unusual safe. Each of the buttons must be pressed only once in the correct order to open it. The last button is marked F. The number of moves and the direction is marked on each button. Thus 1U would mean one move up, while 1L would mean one move to the left. Using the grid reference, which button is the first you must press?

TEST 8 time limit 1 hour

TEST 8

15 Which of the constructed boxes can be made from the pattern?

16 When rearranged the shapes will give a number. Which of the numbers is it?

17 Move from ring to touching ring, starting from the bottom left corner and finishing in the top right corner. Collect nine numbers and total them. Which is the highest possible total?

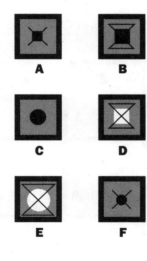

18 Which of the boxes should be used to replace the question mark?

TEST 8 time limit 1 hour

TEST 8

19 Which of the slices should be used to complete the cake so that the top half matches the bottom half?

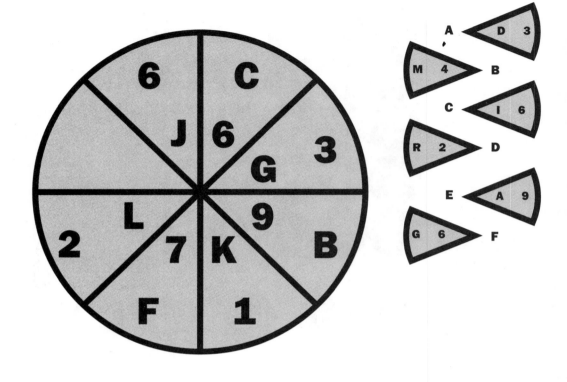

20 Which square's contents matches D2?

21 When the tiles in this square are rearranged a logical pattern will emerge. Which of the tiles should be used to complete the square?

22 Discover the connection between the letters and the numbers. Which number should replace the question mark?

TEST 8 time limit 1 hour

TEST 8

23 Here is an unusual safe. Each of the buttons must be pressed only once in the correct order to open it. The last button is marked F. The number of moves and the direction is marked on each button. Thus 1i would mean one move in, while 1o would mean one move out. 1c would mean one move clockwise and 1a would mean one move anti-clockwise. Which button is the first you must press?

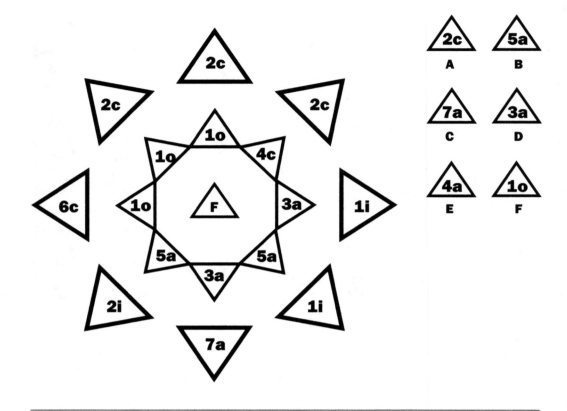

24 Which of the clocks continues this series?

TEST 8 time limit 1 hour

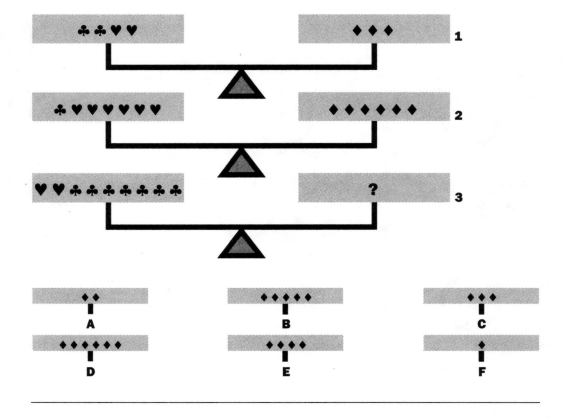

25 Start at 2 and move from circle to touching circle. Collect four numbers each time. How many different routes are there to collect 39? A reversed route counts twice.

26 Scales one and two are in perfect balance. Which of these pans should replace the empty one?

TEST 8 time limit 1 hour

TEST 8

27 Which shape is missing from this series?

28 Which circle should replace the empty one?

TEST 8 time limit 1 hour

29 Which triangle continues this series?

| 53 | | 35 | | 2 | | 4 | | 16 | = | 4 |

30 Insert the correct mathematical signs between each number in order to resolve the equation. What are the signs?

A: ✕ ✕ ✕ ÷

B: + − ✕ ✕

C: − − ✕ ÷

D: − + − ✕

E: ÷ ✕ − −

F: + − ✕ ÷

TEST 8 time limit 1 hour

TEST 1 ANSWERS

1 F. On each row A + B + C = D.

2 D. Ω=5, Ξ=2, Ψ=4, Z=3.

3 F.

4 E.

5 B. The numbers in the first triangle total 3, the second 4 and so on.

6 B. The alphabetical value of each letter is placed next to it.

7 C.

8 C. Each row totals 10.

9 B. The hour hand moves forward two hours each time.

10 E.

11 F.

12 D. When completed the box reads the same both down and across.

13 C.

14 D.

15 F.

SCORE	I.Q.	PERCENTILE
15	130	90
14	125	85
13	122	80
12	117	75
11	115	70
10	112	65
9	108	60
8	105	55
7	100	50
6	95	45
5	90	40

TEST 2 ANSWERS

1 F.

2 A. ♣ = 6, ♥ = 5, ♦ = 2.

3 F.

4 E.

5 C. Each double section totals 10.

6 B. Two series lead from 1 to 16.

7 C.

8 D. Deduct row 2 from row 1 to give row 3.

9 C.

10 E.

11 E. On each row the two squares to the left total 9, as do the two to the right.

12 F. The numbers in the triangles total 4, 6, 8, 10 etc.

13 C.

14 A. The alphabetical value of each letter is placed next to it.

15 A.

SCORE	I.Q.	PERCENTILE
15	130	90
14	125	85
13	122	80
12	117	75
11	115	70
10	112	65
9	108	60
8	105	55
7	100	50
6	95	45
5	90	40

TEST 3 ANSWERS

1   C. $\alpha=4$, $\beta=7$, $\chi=5$, $\delta=8$.

2   A. ♣ = 2, ♥ = 1, ♦ = 3.

3   E.

4   B. Each of the four columns of numbers totals 15.

5   C. 4a in the inner ring.

6   D. The numbers on each row total 9.

7   A. A large triangle added to the nearest small triangle will give the middle number.

8   E. Each double section is added together. Reading clockwise from 2 + 1, the totals increase by one each time.

9   B.

10   E.

11   D.

12   F. Each double section totals 13.

13   A. On each row the first figure minus the second figure plus the third figure gives the fourth.

14   E.

15   E. The first row plus the second row gives the third row.

16   C. The box now reads the same down and across.

17   B.

18   E.

19   E. ♣ = 8, ♥ = 6, ♦ = 7.

20   D. The hour hand moves forward two hours, then three hours, then four hours etc.

SCORE	I.Q.	PERCENTILE
20	138	95
19	136	94
18	134	93
17	132	92
16	131	91
15	130	90
14	125	85
13	122	80
12	117	75
11	115	70
10	112	65
9	108	60
8	105	55
7	100	50
6	95	45
5	90	40

TEST 4 ANSWERS

1 A.

2 B.

3 B. In each triangle the bottom two numbers, when added together, give the top number.

4 F. The hour hand moves back four hours each time.

5 C. On each row A + B - C = D.

6 E.

7 D.

8 A. When completed the box reads the same both down and across.

9 C.

10 C.

11 D.

12 D.

13 A. $\alpha=6$, $\beta=3$, $\chi=7$, $\delta=10$.

14 B.

15 D.

16 F. A large circle minus the nearest small circle will give the middle number.

17 A.

18 B. Reading clockwise, the numbers relate to the number of line forming the shape in the previous sector.

19 C. The first row plus the third row gives the second row. in the middle.

20 E. The alphabetical positions of the letters are placed together in the middle.

SCORE	I.Q.	PERCENTILE
20	138	95
19	136	94
18	134	93
17	132	92
16	131	91
15	130	90
14	125	85
13	122	80
12	117	75
11	115	70
10	112	65
9	108	60
8	105	55
7	100	50
6	95	45
5	90	40

TEST 5 ANSWERS

1 B. 2c in the inner ring.

2 B.

3 A. Reading clockwise, the number in the sector is the alphabetical value of the letter in the previous sector.

4 F.

5 F.

6 C. Each column totals 8.

7 E.

8 B. From the 1, the numbers increase in a spiral by missing out one number, then two numbers, then three numbers and so on.

9 C.

10 F.

11 B. Each double section is added together. These totals increase by two each time.

12 F. When completed the box reads the same both down and across.

13 D. The value of individual letters is irrelevant. The total of the row of numbers must match the total of the column of numbers.

14 E.

15 A.

16 E. On each row A - B - C = D.

17 B.

18 C. ♣ = 4, ♥ = 3, ♦ = 1.

19 D. 1o in the inner ring, between another 1o and 5a.

20 F.

21 A. The left number plus the top number gives the right number in each triangle.

22 C. The alphabetical values of the letters are added to give the number in the middle space.

23 B. The minute hand moves forward ten minutes and the hour hand one hour on each clock.

24 F. Divide the square into four 2 x 2 blocks. The four numbers in each block total 20.

25 D.

26 A.

27 D.

28 A.

29 A.

30 E.

SCORE	I.Q.	PERCENTILE
30	161	99
29	160	99
28	157	99
27	155	99
26	154	98
25	152	98
24	150	98
23	148	98*
22	143	97
21	140	96
20	138	95
19	136	94
18	134	93
17	132	92
16	131	91
15	130	90
14	125	85
13	122	80
12	117	75
11	115	70
10	112	65
9	108	60
8	105	55
7	100	50
6	95	45
5	90	40

*** MENSA LEVEL
You should attempt to join
– see front page for details.**

TEST 6 ANSWERS

1 E. The sectors in the bottom half total one higher than their opposite in the top half.
2 C.
3 F.
4 B.
5 F. 2c in the inner ring with 2c on either side, and 2c outside.
6 D. ♣ = 5, ♥ = 7, ♦ = 4.
7 F.
8 F. The third row plus the second row gives the first row.
9 A. Start in the extreme left circle. The series of arrows zigzags up and down with the arrows pointing as follows: up, down, right, left, down. This repeats.
10 D.
11 B. When completed the box shows the same pattern both down and across.
12 F.
13 C.
14 A. Each double section is added together. This double and its opposite have the same total.
15 E. The middle circle and the two rings of circles all total 24.
16 D.
17 E. The alphabetical positions of the letters are found and the smaller is taken from the larger.
18 C. In each triangle the bottom two numbers are multiplied to give the top.
19 B. K=11, Λ=12, O=15, Π=16.
20 D. On each row A x B + C = D.
21 E. The hour hand moves forward one hour and the minute hand moves five minutes back each time.
22 E.
23 B. Opposite sectors total the same.
24 D.
25 B.
26 B.

27 C.
28 D.
29 C. Start in the top circle. The series of arrows zigzags across in a downward direction with the arrows pointing as follows: right, left, up, up, down, left. This repeats.
30 E.

SCORE	I.Q.	PERCENTILE
30	161	99
29	160	99
28	157	99
27	155	99
26	154	98
25	152	98
24	150	98
23	148	98*
22	143	97
21	140	96
20	138	95
19	136	94
18	134	93
17	132	92
16	131	91
15	130	90
14	125	85
13	122	80
12	117	75
11	115	70
10	112	65
9	108	60
8	105	55
7	100	50
6	95	45
5	90	40

* MENSA LEVEL
You should attempt to join
– see front page for details.

TEST 7 ANSWERS

1 D. The left number divided by the top number gives the right number in each triangle.

2 A.

3 E. The first row plus the second row gives the third row.

4 C. Each double section is added together. All double sections total 9.

5 E.

6 D.

7 D.

8 A. Reverse each row of numbers. Add the second row to the third to give the first row.

9 B.

10 D. When completed the box reads the same both down and across.

11 C.

12 C.

13 F.

14 A. All straight lines of five triangles total 22.

15 E.

16 D.

17 E. In each triangle the left number increases by four, the right number decreases by three and the number at the top doubles each time.

18 D.

19 E.

20 A. 2a in the inner ring, between 1o and 1i.

21 C. φ=6, γ=7, η=8, τ=20.

22 E. When completed the box shows the same pattern both down and across.

23 D.

24 C. ♣ = 1, ♥ = 8, ♦ = 11.

25 E.

26 A. On each row A x B - C = D.

27 D.

28 F.

29 F. The alphabetical values of the letters are placed on opposite sides in the middle space.

30 C. The minute hand moves forward fifteen minutes and the hour hand moves back two hours on each clock.

SCORE	I.Q.	PERCENTILE
30	161	99
29	160	99
28	157	99
27	155	99
26	154	98
25	152	98
24	150	98
23	148	98*
22	143	97
21	140	96
20	138	95
19	136	94
18	134	93
17	132	92
16	131	91
15	130	90
14	125	85
13	122	80
12	117	75
11	115	70
10	112	65
9	108	60
8	105	55
7	100	50
6	95	45
5	90	40

* MENSA LEVEL
You should attempt to join
– see front page for details.

TEST 8 ANSWERS

1 D. Each double section is added together. Totals of opposite sections are equal.
2 C.
3 E.
4 F. Reverse each row of numbers. Add the first row to the second to give the third row.
5 C. 2a in the inner ring between 2a and 1o.
6 C.
7 A. Reverse the alphabet and give each letter its value. For example A=26, B = 25.
8 D. The minute hand moves forward twenty-five minutes and the hour hand moves back four hours on each clock.
9 C. On each row A + B ÷ C = D.
10 F. η=8, φ=10, τ=20, ψ=25.
11 B.
12 E. ♣ = 7, ♥ = 5, ♦ = 9.
13 E. B=2, H=8, N=14, V=22.
14 D.
15 E.
16 B.
17 A.
18 E.
19 C. Give the letters their value in the alphabet and add them to the numbers. The top half of the circle will total 50, as will the bottom half.
20 E.
21 C. When completed the box reads the same both down and across.
22 D. The alphabetical value of the letters to the right are subtracted from the left to give the number in the middle space.
23 D. 3a in the inner ring, with 5a on both sides.
24 A. The minute hand moves back five minutes, then ten minutes then fifteen and so on. The hour hand moves two forward, two back, two forward and so on.
25 B.
26 D. ♣ = 6, ♥ = 9, ♦ = 10.
27 A.
28 F. The number in the middle circle multiplied by the adjacent small circle gives the value in the large outer circle.
29 D. In each triangle the left number decreases by five, four, three, two and so on. The right number increases by three, four, five, six and so on. The number at the top is left plus right.
30 C.

SCORE	I.Q.	PERCENTILE
30	161	99
29	160	99
28	157	99
27	155	99
26	154	98
25	152	98
24	150	98
23	148	98*
22	143	97
21	140	96
20	138	95
19	136	94
18	134	93
17	132	92
16	131	91
15	130	90
14	125	85
13	122	80
12	117	75
11	115	70
10	112	65
9	108	60
8	105	55
7	100	50
6	95	45
5	90	40

* MENSA LEVEL
You should attempt to join
– see front page for details.